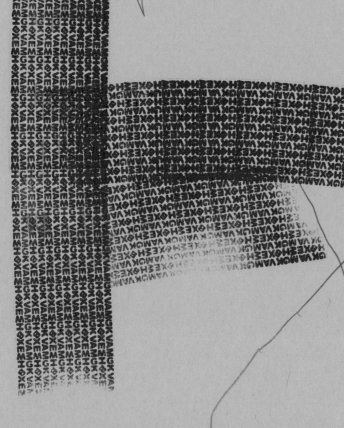

Turtles

Written by Janet Craig
Illustrated by Kathie Kelleher

Troll Associates

Library of Congress Cataloging in Publication Data

Craig, Janet.
    Turtles.

    (Now I know)
    Summary: Brief text and pictures introduce the
turtle, the animal that carries its home on its
back.
    1. Turtles—Juvenile literature.   [1. Turtles]
I. Kelleher, Kathie, ill.   II. Title.
QL666.C5C73   597.92   81-11448
ISBN 0-89375-664-4   AACR2
ISBN 0-89375-665-2 (pbk.)

Which animal carries its home on its back?
Do you know?

The turtle does.

There are many kinds of turtles.

Some live on land.

Here comes the biggest land turtle.

It's the tortoise.

The box turtle lives in the woods.
Like most turtles, its shell is hard.

Its pretty shell is black and orange.

Right now, the box turtle doesn't feel like visiting.

Some turtles live in ponds.

This snapping turtle's shell is small.
But its mouth is big!

Turtles have no teeth.
Their strong beaks help them eat.

Some turtles live in the ocean.

This sea turtle has flippers instead of feet.
Slowly, it swims along.

Baby turtles hatch from eggs.
The mother buries the eggs on land.

The sun warms the eggs.

These eggs are ready to hatch.

Here come the babies!

Off they go to find water.

There are many kinds of turtles. Some live in water.

Some live on land.

But they all carry a home on their backs!